25 MINI-LESSONS FOR TEACHING WRITING

Quick Lessons That Help Students Become Effective Writers

By Adele Fiderer

SCHOLASTIC
PROFESSIONAL BOOKS

NEW YORK · TORONTO · LONDON · AUCKLAND · SYDNEY

ACKNOWLEDGMENTS

I dedicate this book to the teachers of Scarsdale Public Schools
who invited me into their classrooms,
and to all the students who showed us what was possible.

I thank Terry Cooper, who suggested this book,
and Wendy Murray, my editor.

Cover design by Kathy Massaro
Cover photograph by Joan Beard
Interior design by Solutions by Design, Inc.
Interior photographs by Joan Beard; photograph on
page 65 by Catlina Genovese.

ISBN 0-590-20940-X

Table of Contents

Introduction

"Most of my students can't seem to express their feelings and ideas clearly and concisely in writing." If you are like me and most teachers I know, you may be thinking this as you read your students' first pieces of writing in the fall. But here's the good news: Given regular opportunities to write and brief lessons on the techniques that good writers use, our students can become more effective writers.

The mini-lessons in this book will focus on the elements of good writing. They provide practical teaching suggestions to introduce particular elements and strategies, as well as activities that will allow your students to practice the new techniques.

What Makes Writing Good?

The following list, adapted from the ideas of writing expert Donald Murray, includes the elements most commonly identified by experienced writers and teachers of writing as essential for good writing in every form of composition, including personal narrative, fiction, poetry, and content-area writing.

Good writing has:

- **Meaning**
  The writing grows out of experiences and ideas that the writer knows and cares about.

- **Organization**
  It is organized around a limited and clearly defined focus. It has an effective beginning, a logically ordered sequence of events or ideas, and a satisfying ending.

- **Development**
  The information is relevant and sufficient. Supporting reasons and concrete, visual details demonstrate the writer's knowledge of the subject.

- **Clear, Precise Language**
  Good writing is concise and contains few unnecessary words or repetitions. Strong action verbs and specific nouns clearly show the reader what is happening.

- ◎ **Conventions and Mechanics**
  The writing exhibits appropriate usage, spelling, and the mechanics of punctuation, capitalization, and indentation of paragraphs.

Tips for Using and Extending the Mini-lessons

1 Provide your students with lots of good books by their favorite authors. Books can be wonderful resources for good writing techniques.

2 You will need an overhead projector or a photocopier to present most of the activities.

3 See the "Follow-It-Up" pages for each writing element for ways your students can try out a new technique during their regular reading and writing times.

4 When time is short, have your students complete the mini-lesson activity for homework.

How to Create Your Own Mini-lessons

- ◎ Prepare a separate folder for each of the qualities of good writing.

- ◎ When you come across an example of a particular element of good writing in a book, magazine, newspaper, or student's writing, photocopy it and place it in the appropriate folder.

- ◎ Use index cards to jot down any good mini-lesson ideas that you obtain from professional books, workshops, or colleagues. Add these cards to your folders.

- ◎ Encourage your students to look for and share examples of good writing from their favorite books and their own writings. Photocopy the excerpts onto a transparency for overhead projection.

Extending Mini-lesson Strategies

Follow up your mini-lessons on the elements of good writing in class literature discussions and during writing conferences students have with you or with classmates. The sections in this book titled "Follow-It-Up" suggest ideas for connecting writing and literature and for helping your students use mini-lesson strategies to improve their writing.

Meaning

Much like you and me, children find that getting started is the hardest part of writing. One of the best ways to help them leap over this hurdle is to show them how to uncover writing topics they really care about. In this section you will find several techniques that help students mine their daily lives for meaningful stories. The mini-lessons and student activities encourage children to hunt for writing ideas using drawings, time lines, and writer's notebooks.

MINI-LESSON
Find a Topic That Matters

Purpose To help students find interesting stories in their own experiences

Materials
- Story Bank (pages 81–96)
- Individual copies of Student Activity 1 (page 9)

Teaching the Lesson

Select two or three stories from the Story Bank to read to your students. Introduce them by saying something like this: "Listen to these stories written by children. They tell us something important about where writers get their ideas. As you listen, think about where the children's story ideas came from."

After reading the stories, ask the following questions (possible responses in italics):

1. Where did these writers get ideas for their stories?
   From something that really happened to them; from their own lives.

2. Why do you think each writer chose that one particular time to write about?
   It was important, special; a good time; a bad time.

3. What do you think made the writers remember so many things about that special time in their lives?
   Strong feelings: e.g., angry, happy, scared, jealous, proud.

Distribute copies of Student Activity 1 and read the directions aloud to your students.

Name _____ Date _____

Finding the Stories in My Life

Directions:

1. Think about four events in your life that you'll probably never forget. (Hint: Try to remember times when you felt scared, happy, angry, or proud.)

2. Write about the main idea of each story in the boxes below.

3. Decide which story you will write about first. Make a check next to it.

MINI-LESSON
Search for a Topic

Purposes To help students identify important events in their lives

To help students begin keeping folders of writing ideas

Materials ◎ Completed forms of Student Activity 1 (page 9)

◎ Individual copies of Student Activity 2 (page 11)

◎ An oaktag or construction-paper folder for each student

Teaching the Lesson

Call on several volunteers to share the story ideas they selected for Student Activity 1.

Say something like this: "Coming up with a story idea is usually the hardest part of writing. For this reason writers usually try to gather lots of story ideas in folders or notebooks until they are ready to write. These folders will give you a head start when you search for something to write about."

Distribute the writing folders and Student Activity 2.

Name _____ Date _____

Creating a Time Line

Writers write best when they write about things and people they know. Creating a time line of your own life—with important experiences and people recorded on it—can help you come up with good writing ideas.

Look at this time line of Matt's life. The numbers represent years. They cover the year of his birth up to the current year. Matt wrote phrases above and below the number line that tell about events, people, and things that were important to him at different times in his life.

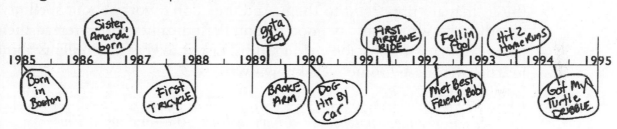

On a separate sheet of unlined paper, make a time line of your own life. Look at Matt's to see how to begin.

1. On the right-hand side of your time line, write the current year.

2. Then go backward in time, filling in the years. The year you were born will be at the left-hand side of the time line. You may not have to use the entire line.

3. Write words or phrases above and below the line that tell about the important events in your life.

4. Draw a line from the words to the time line to indicate the year in which each event occurred.

5. Place your finished time line and Student Activity 1 (Finding the Stories in My Life) in your writing folder. Refer to them whenever you need a good idea for a writing topic.

Which events do you remember best? Think about which one would make an interesting story. Write a title for that story here:

_____

MINI-LESSON
A Writer's Notebook

3

Purpose To demonstrate the importance of journal writing for writers

Materials
◉ Several different types and sizes of notebooks
◉ Individual copies of Student Activity 3 (pages 13–14)

Teaching the Lesson

Explain journal and notebook writing by saying something like this: "Many authors keep journals in which they record their memories, observations, feelings, and story ideas. They write just for themselves about things that are important to them. And they don't worry about spelling or whether the writing is any good or not. Periodically, writers reread their journal entries to look for writing ideas. Listen to these comments about journal writing by some well-known writers:

Jack Prelutsky writes:

> *I save all my ideas notebooks—I have at least 50 —and when I'm ready to write another book of poems I start working my way through all the notebooks. . .*

> (From *How Writers Write* edited by Pamela Lloyd, Heinemann, 1989)

Here's what Roald Dahl had to say about his notebook:

> *I have had this book ever since I started to write seriously. There are 98 pages in the book . . . .And just about every one of them is filled up on both sides with these so-called story ideas. . . .*

> (From *Meet the Authors and Illustrators*, Scholastic, 1991)

And listen to just how important Eve Merriam's notebook is to her:

> *I always have a notebook, always. . . .by my bed. I never travel, even to the post office without a notebook in my hand. . . . . I once got caught without a notebook and it was just painful for me to have to walk all the way home and do nothing but chant over those couple of words I had [in my head].*

> (From *The New Advocate*, Summer 1989)

Display some notebooks in various sizes, with soft and hard covers and various bindings (spiral, stitched, looseleaf).

Distribute copies of Student Activity 3, which should be assigned for homework. Have students fill in the date they must bring the notebook for that activity to school.

Name _____ Date _____

My Writer's Notebook

Directions:

1. Buy a notebook or make your own. Print your name on the cover.

2. Optional: Decorate the cover with words, drawings, cutout pictures, fabric, or contact paper in a way that shows your personality and interests. For example, if you are a baseball fan, you might write, draw, or paste on your cover a picture of your favorite player, game tickets, trading cards, and baseball terms.

3. Write a notebook entry on the first page. Begin by writing the date. Don't worry about spelling, but write clearly enough for your teacher to understand what you have written.

4. If you have trouble thinking of something to write about, use one of the following starters to get your ideas going:

   I was really proud the first time I . . .

   I remember . . .

   Things my parents always say . . .

   My favorite place is . . .

   Someone (or something) I miss a lot is . . .

   I wish that . . .

   I'm really good at . . .

   I'll never forget . . .

   Someone really special to me is . . .

   The most important thing . . .

   This is a family story someone told me . . .

(continued)

5. More suggestions for notebook writing:

⊛ Write a "Things I Love" list.

⊛ Write a "Things I Hate" list.

⊛ Punch a small hole in an index card with a pen. Look through the hole to focus on some object, such as a favorite piece of clothing, a food you love or hate, a special possession—even the inside of a drawer or your closet. Look for the smallest details—such as designs, lines, colors, shapes, markings—and record your observations.

6. SAVE THESE PAGES. Fold them carefully and staple or tape them in your notebook. Look at them again if you're ever stuck for a notebook writing idea.

Meaning: Follow-It-Up

Writing

◎ For writing conferences, have children reread their notebooks to find three entries that might make the most interesting stories. Suggest that they tab those pages with sticky notes, then ask you or a conference partner to help them select a single topic to write about. Ask questions such as the following to help students select a meaningful topic:

I think you may have something interesting here. Can you tell me more about it?

When you think back to this experience, what else do you remember? Why was it special for you?

◎ Encourage your students to reread their notebooks to look for entries that relate to similar subjects or ideas. Then have them develop a writing piece by connecting the entries.

◎ Have your students reread their notebooks periodically to look for word pictures and beautiful language that they can share with you or their classmates.

Literature

During Literature time, read aloud picture books that portray situations and themes that will stimulate memories of people, places, and events. Following each reading, have your students recall word pictures and beautiful language from the book. Then ask your students to write in their notebooks about the memories the book brought to mind, using word pictures and powerful language.

The following are just a few examples of memoir picture books that appeal to middle- and upper-elementary students:

Home Place by Crescent Dragonwagon (Macmillan, 1990)

The Rag Coat by Lauren Mills (Little, Brown, 1991)

Always Grandma by Vaunda Michaux Nelson (Putnam, 1988)

No Star Nights by Anna Egan Smucker (Knopf, 1989)

Home (HarperCollins, 1992), an anthology of essays and poems by 13 well-known authors of children's books

Organization

Early in September, Tony, a fourth-grade teacher I know, announced, "I will positively forbid vacation stories. I don't think I can stand another piece that includes the packing, the car trip, and every sight visited. They're so boring!" Often, a subject is too broad because the writers want to include everything they know about it. Use the mini-lessons and student activities in this section to show your students how to narrow down their "too-big" ideas to focused topics. Then they will learn to brainstorm rich details about that topic, and organize them into paragraphs that build from beginning to middle to end.

MINI-LESSON
Find the Focus

Purpose To demonstrate how a focused, limited subject can improve a story

Teaching the Lesson

Tell your students that you will read aloud two versions of a story written by a fourth grader.

Explain the terms *focused* and *unfocused* by saying: "The first version of Jeff's story tells a little about a lot of different things. We'll call this kind of writing 'unfocused.' The second version zooms in on one small part of the big story and tells a lot about that part. We call this kind of writing 'focused.' As you listen, think about the differences between an unfocused and a focused story."

My Trip to California (unfocused)

I went to California with my parents and my sister. The plane ride to California was boring. First we went to Palm Springs, where my grandparents live. On Friday we drove to Disneyland. That was great! We were staying at the Marriott Hotel in Los Angeles. That night we went out to dinner with my cousins who live there. When we got back to the hotel, my sister and I went up to our room on the elevator and my parents and cousins stayed downstairs in the lobby. My sister and I were sitting on our beds in our room watching two men bobsledding in the Olympics, and all of a sudden a really deep and loud honking noise went off. It was a fire alarm. We were scared till the porter told us it was a false alarm.

The Scare at the Marriott (focused)

My sister and I were sitting on our beds in our room at the Marriott Hotel in Los Angeles watching TV. Two men were bobsledding in the Olympics when, all of a sudden, a really deep, loud honking noise went off. At first I thought it was the pipes in the bathroom. Then I thought it was a fire alarm. I was shaking. I opened the door and saw a couple of people in the hall. This one lady had hair curlers on and a light blue nightgown that came over her knees. She ran around the corner like she was going to have a heart attack. Then the noise stopped.

The lady came back and said out loud, "It's a fire alarm, just like on the ship."

My sister said to me, "What ship?"

I was really puzzled about everything until a porter came by and said it was a false alarm. We went back to watching TV. By that time bobsledding was over and figure skating was just about to start.

Compare Focused and Unfocused Versions

After the reading, have your students comment on the differences between the focused and unfocused versions. Record their comments on a chart or overhead transparency using the following organizer. [Possible student responses are shown in italics.]

Version 1—Unfocused	Version 2—Focused
just a list of things	*more interesting*
boring	*scary and funny*
told about too many places	*showed what was happening*
	people were talking

5 MINI-LESSON
Limit the Topic

Purpose To extend the preceding lesson by providing additional practice in recognizing and narrowing an unfocused topic

Material ◉ Student Activity 5 (pages 21–22)

Teaching the Lesson

Help students recall the unfocused version of Jeff's story about his trip to California (see Mini-lesson 4) by saying something like this: "First Jeff wrote about many different things he and his family did on their trip to California. He told about the plane ride, visiting his grandparents, driving to Disneyland, going to dinner with his cousins, and about the alarm going off when he and his sister were watching the Olympics on TV. Most of you thought that this kind of 'list' wasn't really interesting.

"I thought that Jeff's second version, which focused on the night the hotel's alarm went off, was a more interesting story. Who remembers some of the details he gave us so that we could see how scary and funny that experience was?"

Call on students to contribute details, and supply any they omit.

Then ask, "What other parts of the trip to California might Jeff have chosen to focus on?"

If someone suggests "Disneyland," point out that Jeff might end up with another "list" story if he just wrote about all the rides he went on in the amusement park. Ask for suggestions about how Jeff could avoid that problem by limiting his subject even further.[Possible responses: *Write about the most exciting or most boring ride he went on. Write about something funny or scary that happened at the park.*]

Distribute Student Activity 5. [Answers: *Numbers 1, 3, and 4 zoom in on a united, focused topic.*]

MINI-LESSON
Focus with a Topic Web

Purpose To demonstrate how to construct a topic web

Material ◉ Individual copies of Student Activity 6 (page 23)

Teaching the Lesson

Ask your students to think again about Jeff's first attempt to write about his trip to California (or reread his first draft in Mini-lesson 4 on page 18). Explain that one way Jeff could have dealt with the problem of having too big a topic would have been to break down his broad subject into specific, individual topics. On the chalkboard draw an outline of a topic web (see Student Activity 6).

1 Write "Trip to California" inside the web's central oval.

2 Ask students to suggest subtopics—the little stories that Jeff might have chosen as a focus for his writing.

3 As ideas are offered, write them in surrounding ovals and connect them to the central one.

4 Tell your students that they will now have the opportunity to create their own topic web. Distribute copies of Student Activity 6.

Look for Limited Topics

Directions: Read the following stories. Place a check beside the ones that zoom in on a limited, focused topic.

_____ **#1 MR. FIX-IT**

When I was three years old, I liked cars and trucks. Once I took the Toyota's motor apart while my mom was doing the laundry. I climbed over the small fence in front of our house. I got my grandfather's tools. It was 11:00. I worked and worked and soon I was done. At 4:00 my grandfather came home from work. I got a spanking. After my mom picked up my sister at school, everybody tried to fix the car's motor. Nobody could fix it. So we had to give it back to the dealer and we got a new car.

Bobby, grade 3

_____ **#2 WHEN I WENT TO CANADA**

I went to Canada with my family. First we went to the glass museum. Five hours later, we went to Rochester. We slept there. The next day we went to Niagara Falls. We rode the boat. I was scared because the boat went in front of the falls and I got so wet. We drove to Niagara-on-the-Lake and we went to the store and we slept in a hotel.

Sally, grade 3

_____ **#3 THE BAD RAINY DAY**

One day it was rainy and windy out. A tree fell on our school. It was an old tree. It didn't damage the school because that part of the building was made of brick. The playground was closed because part of the tree was on the slide. Some of the

(continued)

branches had smashed the windows. The next day it was rainy again and another tree fell down. The custodians chopped up the trees. Then they put them on the truck and took them away.

Jeffrey, grade 3

____ #4 THE ACCIDENT

I had one slice of pizza in one hand and my other slice of pizza in the other hand. I put my soda under my arm. I was walking slow. As I was on the way to my table, a man was getting up, and his shoulder bumped into my arm and knocked the soda bottle down on the floor. It splashed my face and my clothes. I looked like a monster. Then I went to the bathroom to clean myself up. I got out fast because I wanted to eat my pizza.

John, grade 4

____ #5 DISNEYLAND

When my family and I went to Disneyland in California, I went on Space Mountain. It was fast. I also went on Pirates of the Caribbean and the Haunted House. My sister liked Mickey's Treehouse. On Runaway Train, I saw dinosaur bones that squirted water. On Star Wars, I liked R2D2 and C3PO. The driver took us in space on his first drive. We saw a movie and the seats went sideways and up and down.

Lincoln, grade 3

STUDENT ACTIVITY 6

Using a Topic Web

Directions: Make a topic web for any of the following "too-big" topics, or use your own idea:

My Trip to _____

My Favorite TV Shows

My Friends

My Family

My Favorite Games and Sports

_____

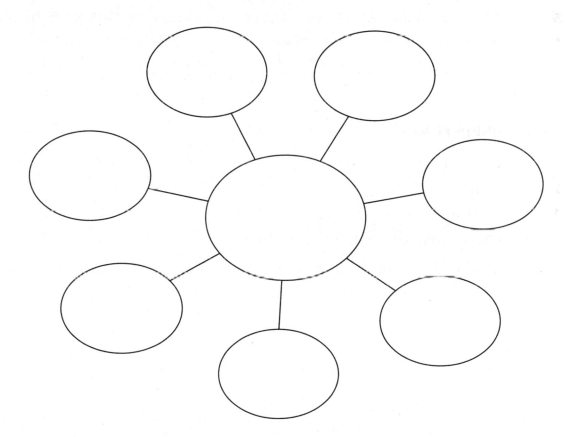

Now choose one of the topics you've listed and on a separate sheet of paper, write that topic in the center of a web. Brainstorm details and events that go with that topic. Doing this well help you discover focused story ideas.

MINI-LESSON

Let the Title Show the Focus

Purpose To show how titles often reflect the focus (unifying idea) of a story

Material ◎ Individual copies of Student Activity 7 (page 25)

Teaching the Lesson

Help your students recall Jeff's titles for the two versions of his story: "My Trip to California" and "A Scare at the Marriott" (Mini-lesson 4, page 18). Point out that a title often gives the reader a clue about whether a story will be focused or unfocused.

Copy the following pair of titles on the chalkboard. Ask, "Which title shows that the writer has focused on a small, sharp, clear subject?"

Title 1: Cooking Pancakes with Grandma

Title 2: My Relatives

Point out to your students that "Cooking Pancakes with Grandma" could be a chapter in a book called *My Relatives*. Encourage them to think about writing a chapter at a time when they have too broad a subject.

Distribute Student Activity 7 (page 25). [Answers: A. 1. b; 2. b; 3. a; 4. a; 5. a; 6. a; 7. b. B: Answers will vary.]

Find the Titles that Show a Focus

A. Directions: Read the following pairs of titles. Check the title in each pair that best focuses on a small, sharp, clear subject.

1. _____ a) Horses
   _____ b) Getting Stepped on by My Own Horse

2. _____ a) Kids in My Class
   _____ b) Archer the Burper

3. _____ a) Getting Splashed on Space Mountain
   _____ b) A Day in Disneyland

4. _____ a) My Collection of Baseball Cards
   _____ b) My Hobbies

5. _____ a) My favorite baseball card
   _____ b) My Collection of Baseball Cards

6. _____ a) Trying the High Dive
   _____ b) A Day at the Pool

7. _____ a) My Best Memories
   _____ b) My First Bike Ride

B. Directions: Write titles that would limit the following "too-big" topics. (Hint: Choose the one thing that you could write a lot about.)

1. _____ a) My Favorite Things
   _____ b) _____

2. _____ a) How I Spent My Summer Vacation
   _____ b) _____

3. _____ a) My Relatives
   _____ b) _____

Focus: Follow-It-Up

Writing

◎ Ask students to create two or more alternative titles for stories they are writing or planning to write. Then have them work in pairs to select the title that best shows the focus of their story.

◎ Before students begin to write a new piece, have them develop several possible titles. Ask them to choose the title that will help them focus on a small, clear subject.

◎ During a writing conference, respond to an unfocused draft with comments such as the following:

You tell about so many different things here. Which one part was really special? How come? Can you tell me more about it?

That sounds interesting. Why not write about that part and include all the details you talked about. Think of a new title that would help you focus.

Literature

◎ After reading aloud a chapter of a story, have students discuss what it was mainly about. Reread the chapter's title and invite students to comment on it and suggest possible alternative titles the author might have used.

8 | MINI-LESSON
How a Story Is Developed

Purpose To demonstrate how writers organize information

Material ◉ Individual copies of Student Activity 8 (pages 28–29)

Teaching the Lesson

Distribute Student Activity 8 and read aloud the story "Learning About Leeches."

Read the directions in Section B aloud. If your students are unfamiliar with the term *paragraph*, explain that a paragraph groups together sentences that are about the same topic.

Ask the following question to help students get started with the paragraph exercise: "If Nicholas found out that barbers also applied leeches to sick people, where would that fact belong?"

[Answers to Student Activity 8: *A. 1. How leeches eat; 2. How leeches were used as medicine. B. (a) 2; (b) 1; (c) 3; (d) 3. Main topic of third paragraph: leech reproduction.*]

Working with Paragraphs

A. Directions: Read 4th-grade Nicholas's story "Learning About Leeches," which follows:

Did you know that leeches and Dracula have something in common? They both suck blood from animals. A leech eats by going to an animal and biting into it with its sharp teeth. It then sucks the blood from the animal. This supplies the leech with the food it needs.

Leeches used to be used as medicine. A doctor would put several leeches on a patient. The leeches would suck the person's blood. People thought that by sucking the person's blood, the leeches would be taking away the disease. This was not a good idea because instead of getting better, people would almost die from losing too much blood, and some did die.

1. What does the first paragraph mainly tell about?

_____

_____

_____

_____

2. What does the second paragraph mainly tell about?

_____

_____

_____

_____

(continued)

B. Directions: Read the following facts about leeches. Write a 1 before each fact that belongs in the first paragraph. Write a 2 before each fact that belongs in the second paragraph. Write a 3 before a fact that doesn't belong in either the first or second paragraph and should be in a third paragraph.

_____ a) Leeches are still used sometimes to prevent blood swellings.

_____ b) Leeches have two sucking mouths, one in front and one in back.

_____ c) Leeches lay their eggs in cases called cocoons.

_____ d) When the young hatch, they attach themselves to the underside of an adult leech and are carried around until they are old enough to be on their own.

What is the main topic of the third paragraph?

_____

_____

_____

MINI-LESSON 9
Focus with a Lead

Purposes To show how leads reflect and direct the focus of a story

To demonstrate how writers experiment with several leads to create an effective beginning

Materials
- An overhead transparency or individual copies of Student Activity 9 (page 31)
- A copy of E. B. White's book *Charlotte's Web* (HarperCollins), if available

Teaching the Lesson

Read aloud, from Student Activity 9, E. B. White's experiments with different beginnings for *Charlotte's Web*.

Ask your students to select or vote for the lead that they would have used to introduce the story.

Read aloud White's final choice, (d). (Reading directly from the book at this point adds drama to this lesson.)

Ask children why they think the author may have chosen that lead.

Discuss the information that each of the leads provides for the reader. [Possible responses: (a) *a description of Wilbur, the main character*; (b and c) *a description of the barn, the setting of the story*; (d) *dialogue that hints at the story's problem*; (e) *actions and dialogue that hint at the problem*; (f) *a description of Charlotte, another main character.*]

Name _____ Date _____

Choose Your Favorite Leads

E. B. White's Lead Experiments for *Charlotte's Web*

Directions: Choose three leads from those below that make you want to read more of the story. Write a 1, 2, and 3 in the blanks next to your first, second, and third choices.

_____ a) "He was what farmers call a spring pig—which simply means that he was born in springtime. He was small, had a good physique, and was generally white and he lived in the cellar."

_____ b) "The warmest and pleasantest part of Zuckerman's barn was the part where the cows were on the south side. It was warm because the sun shone in through the door, and it was warm because of the manure pile."

_____ c) "A barn can have a horse in it, and a barn can have a cow in it, and a barn can have hens scratching in the chaff and swallows flying in and out through the door—but if a barn hasn't got a pig in it, it is hardly worth talking about."

_____ d) "'Where's Papa going with that ax?' said Fern to her mother as they were setting the table for breakfast. 'Out to the hoghouse,' replied Mrs. Arable. 'Some pigs were born last night.'"

(continued)

_____ e) "At midnight, John Arable pulled his boots on, lit a lantern, and walked out through the woods to the hog-house. The sow lay on her side; her eyes were closed. Huddled in a corner stood the newborn pigs, ten of them. . .

'Ten of them,' he murmured. 'Nine full size and one runty pig. Little Wilbur.'"

_____ f) "Charlotte was a big grey spider who lived in a door-way. But there is no use talking about Charlotte until we have talked about her close friend—a pig named Wilbur."

(Leads are from *The Horn Book*, October 1982.) For more of E.B. White's drafts and revision notes, see *The Annotated Charlotte's Web* by Peter Neumeyer, HarperCollins, 1993

MINI-LESSON
Experiment with Leads

Purpose To show how student writers can experiment with leads to find one that will (1) capture the reader's attention and (2) reflect the mood of the story

Material ◎ Individual copies or an overhead transparency of Student Activity 10 (page 34)

Teaching the Lesson

Point out that writers try to create leads that will grab readers. Ask students to think about which leads in Student Activity 10 would make them want to read the story.

Read the leads aloud, one pair at a time. After each reading, have students vote for the lead they prefer. Call on students to offer reasons for their preferences.

Ask students how Todd ("Space Mountain") may have discovered his second lead. [Possible responses: *It was the third sentence. He dropped the first two sentences. He added parts that showed he was scared.*]

Explain that a lead often provides a clue about a story's mood—whether it will be funny, scary, exciting, or sad. Have students reread Lead #2 for each story in Student Activity 10 and discuss the mood and the language that creates it.

Name _____ Date _____

Select the Best Beginnings

Directions: Read the following introductions, or leads. For each story, check the lead that you think works best. Think about what makes it a good introduction.

Space Mountain

___ Lead #1

When I got to Disneyworld, my best and scariest ride was called Space Mountain. Space Mountain is a very, very scary roller coaster. When I saw Space Mountain, I began to shiver. Once I got inside, it looked like I was in another dimension.

___ Lead #2

When I saw Space Mountain at Disneyworld, I began to shiver. Once I got inside, it looked like I was in another dimension. There were screens all over the place. One screen showed what the ride would be like. After I saw it, I said to myself, "Am I really going to go through with this?"

Todd, grade 4

The Noise

___ Lead #1

Yesterday I went to my friend's house and ate lunch there. Just when we were going to leave, we both heard a noise. It came from upstairs. The noise sounded like footsteps. We went upstairs to investigate. My friend ran away from the thudding noise, too.

___ Lead #2

One dark, spooky night I heard a thud while watching the movie *Young Frankenstein*. I thought it came from upstairs. I went to the second floor to investigate. I could not find a thing. I went to the attic. I froze like an icicle.

Emily, grade 5

MINI-LESSON
Great Beginnings:
Writers' Techniques

Purpose To study the techniques that writers use for creating introductions

Material ◎ Individual copies of Student Activity 11 (pages 36–37)

Teaching the Lesson

Ask your students why writers try to create good beginnings for their stories. [Possible responses: *First few sentences help me decide whether to read the book or look for a different one. Tells me what the story will be about. Helps me know if it's my kind of story.*]

Write the following list on a chalkboard or transparency:

Examples of techniques writers use for story leads (beginnings):
◎ Picture or unusual image
◎ Dialogue (could be one person thinking or talking)
◎ Action
◎ Question
◎ Interesting fact

Read aloud the following leads. Ask your students to identify the technique that the writer used.

1 | "Imagine being so good at gymnastics that you could do handstands, backbends, and walkovers—all on the jiggling back of a cantering horse."

(From *American Girl* magazine, July–Aug., 1995)

2 | Did you know cats were mummified in Egypt a long time ago?

[Possible responses: 1. *a picture, an unusual image*; 2. *a question, an interesting fact*.]

Distribute Student Activity 11.
Say: "Choose the letter from the key that identifies each author's technique. Some leads may demonstrate two techniques."

[Answers: *1. D, Q; 2. P; 3. P; 4. D, A; 5. I, Q; 6. A, P.*]

Scholastic Professional Books, 1997

Name _____ Date _____

Tell the Technique

Directions: Choose the letter(s) that identify each writer's technique(s) for creating a great beginning. Write it/them in the blank following each example.

```
┌─────────────────────────────────────┐
│               Key:                   │
│   P = Picture or unusual image       │
│   D = Dialogue                       │
│   A = Action                         │
│   Q = Question                       │
│   I = Interesting fact               │
└─────────────────────────────────────┘
```

1. "When are you going to practice?" Has your mom ever said this to you?

   (From "Piano Lessons" by Charlie, grade 4).

   Technique: _____

2. When my father woke me at six o'clock next morning. I knew at once that this was the day of days. It was the day I longed for and the day I dreaded. It was also the day of butterflies in the stomach, except they were worse than butterflies. They were snakes. I had snakes in the stomach from the moment I opened my eyes on that Friday morning.

   (From *Danny The Champion of the World* by Roald Dahl, Viking Penguin)

   Technique: _____

(continued)

3. It was a gray November afternoon in Michigan's North Woods. Mark Wolfe stood motionless; only his eyes moved as a cold breeze rustled the brown oak leaves overhead and the steam from his breath drifted over his face.

> (From "Buck Fever" by Kendal Taylor, *Cricket Magazine*, Nov. 1989)

Technique: _____

4. "Dribble, Dave, dribble!" I screamed. We were losing the soccer game 2–1 against Fox Meadow. Boy, was I mad."

> (From "A Close Game" by Sadi, grade 6)

Technique: _____

5. Did you know walruses' young when born weigh 100 pounds? They are even born on ice.

> (From "Walruses" by Emily, grade 3)

Technique: _____

6. As slim and straight as an arrow, Donald Bonnette glides over the water with grace and ease, the way a bird glides on currents of air.

> (From "Wizard on Water Skis" by Louis Sabin, *Boys Life Magazine*)

Technique: _____

Great Beginnings: Follow-It-Up

Writing

◎ Explain that most writers do not come up with masterful leads on their first try. A good lead is usually the result of brainstorming and experimentation. Read aloud the following example of a third grader's revision of a lead for a story called "Shamoo":

Lead 1: "When I was in Florida my family and I went to Sea World."

Lead 2: "Shamoo is a fourteen-and-a-half-foot-long killer whale. He is trained to talk."

Then ask your students to reread the beginning of a piece they are currently writing and to develop one or two alternate leads for it. Invite them to read their new leads to the class or to a partner to help them make their final choice.

◎ Create a "Great Beginnings" bulletin board for displaying effective leads written by students and professional authors. Provide markers and oaktag so that students can recopy the leads for the display.

◎ Select leads from the Story Bank (pages 81–96) to read to your students.

◎ Encourage students to share leads from their own writing, and invite classmates to comment on each other's techniques.

Literature

◎ After reading a short story or a book's chapter aloud, reread the lead. Ask: "What did this writer do here to make us want to read on?"

◎ Invite your students to share leads from the stories they read in books, magazines, and newspapers. Everyone should try to identify the specific technique or techniques (action, dialogue, question, interesting fact, etc.) that the writer used to attract readers.

MINI-LESSON
Satisfying Endings

Purpose To study the ways writers end their stories

Materials ◎ Two or three student stories from the Story Bank (pages 81–96) that would be appropriate for your students

◎ Individual copies of Student Activity 12 (page 40)

Teaching the Lesson

Copy the list shown in "Examples of Story-Ending Techniques" from Student Activity 12 onto a chart or overhead transparency.

Explain that today's lesson will focus on techniques writers use to create endings for their stories. Ask your students what they hope to find out when they get to the end of a story. [Possible responses: *how a problem was solved; whether it had a happy or sad ending; how things finally turned out in the end.*]

Point out the following criteria for effective endings:

1 The ending should be connected to the story.

2 It should be interesting—something that the reader will remember.

3 It should tie things up and not leave the reader wondering what happened.

4 It should be brief—just a few sentences.

Tell your students that you will read aloud stories written by children. Remind them to listen to the stories carefully, paying particular attention to the way each writer ended his or her story.

After each reading, ask your students to look at "Examples of Story-Ending Techniques" in Student Activity 12 to help them determine which technique the writer used. If someone suggests a technique that is not on the list, add it.

Distribute Student Activity 12. [Answers: *1. C; 2. D; 3. E; 4. A; 5. B.*]

STUDENT ACTIVITY 12

Examining Story Endings

Directions:

1. Read "Examples of Story-Ending Techniques," below.

2. Read "Students' Story Endings," also below.

3. Find the technique that best describes each ending. Write the letter for that technique in front of the ending.

Examples of Story-Ending Techniques

A. Describes the writer's present thoughts or feelings about a past experience.

B. Tells how the story problem was solved.

C. Tells what the subject of the story—a person, pet, or object — means to the writer.

D. Tells about what happened afterward or predicts something that might happen in the future.

E. Sums things up.

Students' Story Endings

_____ 1. Max is not just a pet, he's a brother. He follows me everywhere if I tell him to. But the most important thing is that we love each other.

_____ 2. After that I never again left my baby brother alone in the house.

_____ 3. Now you know why Amy is my best friend.

_____ 4. Of course, I've calmed down a lot since fifth grade, but whenever I look back on that day I always think, "Why did it have to be me?"

_____ 5. My dad marched up with a screwdriver and the door swung open. "We're free! We're free!" Lauren and I kept yelling. We both ran to my dad and gave him a hug.

Satisfying Endings: Follow-It-Up

Writing

◉ Before they complete their stories, have students pair up and discuss different endings they might write.

◉ After completing a draft of a story, invite several volunteers to rewrite their endings using a different technique. Have these students read aloud their story and its two endings for a class discussion.

◉ During peer writing conferences, suggest that students ask each other, "How do you think you might end this story?" or "Is there another way for the story to end?"

Literature

◉ Have your students reread the ending of a book they have finished to identify the author's technique.

◉ Collect a variety of short picture books that have "twist" endings for your students to enjoy and discuss. For example, *The Frog Prince Continued* by Jon Scieszka (Viking) ends this way: The Prince kissed the Princess. They both turned into frogs. And they hopped off happily ever after.

◉ Read aloud or have your students read nonfiction articles found in magazines and newspapers and discuss the technique that each writer used to create an ending.

◉ After a read-aloud, ask your students to suggest additional endings that the author might have used.

Scholastic Professional Books, 1997

Development

"We had a great time at the park and then we went home."
Have you seen writing like this? I bet you have. Weening
students off of writing sentences that "tell" rather than
"show" the reader what is happening is one of the toughest
challenges in teaching writing. But the mini-lessons in this
chapter will help you do it. They include examples of both
kinds of writing to help your students really see the
difference showing-not-telling can make. They will learn to
use specific information, description, and visual details to
create stories of greater depth and impact.

 **MINI-LESSON**

Writing That Shows

Purpose To demonstrate how students can develop their writing with specific, honest information that shows, rather than tells, the reader what is happening

Material ◉ Individual copies of Student Activity 13 (page 45)

Teaching the Lesson

Demonstrate the difference between writing that shows and writing that tells. First, write on the chalkboard, "The teacher was angry." Then announce that you are going to act like an angry teacher. Begin, for example, by rapping on a desk with a ruler and shouting, "One more sound and everyone stays in for recess!" Stomp to the chalkboard, scowl, fold your arms across your chest, and say, "I heard someone laugh. All right, then, fifty math problems for homework!"

Then—as yourself—turn to your students and ask them to describe your previous words and actions. As they do, write what they say on the chalkboard. (They'll say things such as *You stomped to the chalkboard* and *Your eyebrows jammed together.*) Then read aloud their descriptions. Ask students to compare their description on the board to the original sentence, "The teacher was angry."

Explain to your students that the sentence "The teacher was angry" is writing that *tells.* But their descriptions of your actions show a reader what a character is like and what is happening. Point out that good writers try to *show*—not *tell.*

Distribute Student Activity 13. [Answers: *1. E; 2. C; 3. A; 4. D; 5. B.*]

Show, Don't Tell!

Directions: Match the underlined word in each of the following sentences with its fuller description below the heading "Writing That Shows." (The underlined word *tells*; the matching description *shows*.)

Write the letter of the matching description in the blank before each sentence.

_____ 1. I could hardly wait until my mom came home from the hospital with the new baby. The baby was <u>cute</u>.

_____ 2. My friend and I locked the bedroom door to keep my brother out. When I tried to open it, the doorknob came off in my hand. I tried to jam it back on, but it was hopeless. I was really <u>scared</u> and so was my friend.

_____ 3. It was my aunt's wedding day. She looked really <u>pretty</u>.

_____ 4. The wedding cake was <u>beautiful</u>!

_____ 5. I was going to feed my mother's horse a section of hay. But before I got in the stall, the door slid open and the horse walked out and accidentally <u>knocked me over</u>.

Writing That Shows

A. She was wearing a white silk dress with a pink ribbon around her waist. Her veil was attached to flowers in her hair. (Elizabeth, grade 4)

B. My mother opened the stall slowly. The big, brown pregnant horse Fatalean wobbled out while I charged in. We hit! My

(continued)

head to her chest. I fell to the concrete flat on my stomach.
Fatalean walked right over the top of me. (Jayme, grade 6)

C. I thought I would never get out. Maybe we would be there for
   weeks without food. I looked out the window. I wanted to
   jump. Lauren would not let me. She thought I would kill myself
   because we were on the second floor. (Lauren, grade 4)

D. It said "Stairway to the Stars," and the icing was white with
   brown, green, and yellow decorations. (Elizabeth, grade 4)

E. Melissa has big blue eyes, straight black hair, and soft skin. She
   has red cheeks, too. Her fingers and toes are tiny, and her
   clothes aren't much bigger than a big doll's. (Ed, grade 3)

MINI-LESSON
Show, Don't Tell!
How Authors Do It

Purpose To show how professional writers reveal characters and their feelings

Materials
- Each student should have a familiar book or short story
- Page markers (e.g., sticky notes, index cards, strips of paper)
- An overhead transparency or individual copies of Student Activity 14 (page 49)

Teaching the Lesson

Introduce the lesson by saying something like this: "Many of you have read Harry Allard's book *Miss Nelson is Missing*. Listen to the way Allard shows us what Miss Nelson's kids were like":

> *The kids in Room 207 were misbehaving again. Spitballs stuck to the ceiling. Paper planes whizzed through the air. They were the worst-behaved class in the whole school. . . . They whispered and giggled. They squirmed and made faces. They were even rude during story hour.*

Ask your students how a writer who doesn't know the "Show, Don't Tell" technique might describe the same scene. [Possible responses: *The kids were bad. Miss Nelson's class was terrible.*]

Then read aloud the following passage from Judy Blume's book *The One in the Middle Is the Green Kangaroo*. Remind students to listen carefully to the words that show a reader exactly what Freddy is feeling.

> *It was time for the play to begin. Freddy waited backstage with the fifth and sixth graders who were in the play. They looked at him and smiled. He tried to smile back. But the smile wouldn't come. His heart started to beat faster. His stomach bounced up and down. He felt funny. Then Ms. Matson leaned close to him. She said, "They're waiting for you, Freddy. Go ahead."*

After reading the passage, write "The Feeling" and "Words That Show It" on the board. Have students help you list information from the passage for each category. [Possible responses: The feeling: *fear*. Words That Show It: *His heart started to beat faster. His stomach bounced up and down.*]

Ask, "What might a writer who doesn't know the "Show, Don't Tell" technique have written instead?" [Possible responses: *Freddy was scared. He had stage fright.*]

Distribute copies of Student Activity 14.

Name _____ Date _____

Show, Don't Tell: Word Hunt

Title of Book _____

Author _____

Main Character _____

Directions:

A. Skim through the story you have chosen to hunt for writing that shows what the character is feeling (e.g., scared, happy, lonely, excited, nervous).
   Look for **actions** and **words** that express these feelings.

B. Place a marker on each page that has writing that "shows" the character's feelings.

C. Write the information you have discovered on the following lines:

1. _____ _____
   page   the feeling

   _____
                 words that show it

2. _____ _____
   page   the feeling

   _____
                 words that show it

3. _____ _____
   page   the feeling

   _____
                 words that show it

4. _____ _____
   page   the feeling

   _____
                 words that show it

MINI-LESSON
Develop with Details

Purposes   To learn the importance of details in writing
To develop a topic by adding details

Material   ◉ Student Activity 15 (page 51)

Teaching the Lesson

On the chalkboard write the following sentence: "The storm was awesome."

Then say, "This sentence needs details to put a clearer picture in our minds. For example, I could say something like this: 'The storm was awesome. The wind howled all night long.'"

Ask each student to supply another detail that would show how bad the storm was. Suggest that they use their own memories or imagination to visualize a storm. For example, a student might say, "The storm was awesome; it was so windy that a huge tree in my yard blew down."

Continue to ask around the room until all students who want to have supplied at least one detail. Ask students to try to recall vivid or interesting details suggested by classmates that made them hear the storm or see what it did.

Distribute individual copies of Student Activity 15 or copy the list of sentences onto the chalkboard and read the directions aloud. Provide additional paper for children to illustrate their descriptions with pictures. [You may prefer to ask students to trade descriptions and illustrate a classmate's writing instead of their own.]

Name _____   Date _____

Adding Details

1. The room was a mess.

2. The storm was awesome.

3. He has everything a kid could ask for.

4. It was a spooky night.

5. I played the best game ever.

Directions:

Choose one sentence from the list above and use it to write a short, detailed description below. Begin by writing the sentence you selected. Then add details that will create pictures in a reader's mind.

   When you finish, you may want to draw a picture of the setting or situation based on its description. Include as many visual details from the writing as possible.

_____

_____

_____

_____

_____

_____

_____

_____

Development: Follow-It-Up

Writing

◎ During writing conferences with students, listen for writing that "tells" but doesn't "show." Ask such writers questions like, "You say you were scared. What were you thinking while that was happening?" Or, "Here you wrote that the party was great. What are the things that made it so good?" Encourage students to add the expanded descriptions to their drafts.

◎ Invite your students to share before-and-after revisions that demonstrate how they improved their writing by adding details and descriptions.

◎ Chart conference questions that help writers describe scenes, actions, thoughts, and feelings [e.g., "Can you tell me more about . . . ?"]. Encourage students to ask these questions during a writing conference with a classmate whose writing tells rather than shows readers what is happening.

Literature

◎ Tell your students that writers show what a character is like through the character's actions and words (e.g., kind, cruel, friendly, unfriendly, brave, timid). Then ask them to hunt through books or magazines for examples of writing that reveal a character's temperament. Suggest that they insert strips of paper to mark pages with examples so that they can share them with a partner or the class afterward.

◎ After a read-aloud, invite students to comment on a passage that demonstrated the author's effective use of details to describe a place, character, or event.

Clarity

"Be specific" is advice most student writers need. They should be able to use strong verbs (*tumbled* instead of *fell*) and comparisons (*weak as a baby*) to power their sentences. Children should also learn that if they replace general words such as *lunch* with more specific words—*a peanut-butter and jelly sandwich and a glass of cold milk*—a reader will be able to visualize the scene. The mini-lessons in this section will help your students use language that puts clearer pictures into a reader's mind.

MINI-LESSON
Sharpen the Picture:
How Authors Do It

Purposes To learn the importance of using concrete information
To replace general words with specific words

Material ⊛ Individual copies of Student Activity 16 (page 55)

Teaching the Lesson

Write the following sentences on the chalkboard or an overhead transparency.

> *First try*:
> "Charlotte was a big grey spider who lived in the doorway of a barn."
> *Second try*:
> "Charlotte was a grey spider who lived in the doorway of a barn. She was about the size of a gumdrop and she had eight legs."

Tell your students that the above sentences were written by E. B. White for his book *Charlotte's Web*. Ask them what they notice about the revisions or changes that the writer made in his second try. [Possible responses: *He left out the word "big." He described exactly what she looked like.*]

Then say something like this: "'Big' is a general word. Like E. B. White, all good writers try to use specifics. Listen, for example, to the way Judy Blume uses specific details to describe the materials her characters use to make their school project":

> *We keep our equipment under my bed in a shoe box. We have a set of Magic Markers, Elmer's glue, Scotch tape, a really sharp pair of scissors and a container of silver sparkle.*
>
> (From *Tales of a Fourth Grade Nothing*)

Distribute Student Activity 16 and explain to students that they will practice replacing several words with more specific ones, and vice versa.

[Possible responses to Student Activity 16: A. automobile: *old pick-up truck*; noise: *screeching fire alarm*; TV show: *The Simpsons*; dog: *little terrier*; money: *$5.20*; meat: *a medium-rare steak*; flower: *wilted, pink petunia*; baby: *a two-month-old girl*. B. 1. *While I was home alone watching Star Trek, I heard a thump in the kitchen.* 2. *On Saturday Ray and I rode our bikes to Highland Park. We bought hot dogs and lemonade.* 3. *The soccer ball cost $12.00.*]

Name _____ Date _____

Sharpen With Specifics

Directions:

A. Fill in the blanks in the columns below: If a general word is given, write a more specific word or words in the matching blank. If a specific word or words are listed, fill in the matching blank with a general word for it/them.

	General Words	**Specific Words**
Example:	candy	a Snickers bar
	automobile	_____
	noise	_____
	TV show	_____
	dog	_____
	_____	$5.20
	_____	a medium-rare steak
	flower	_____
	_____	a two-month-old girl

Directions:

B. Some of the general words in the sentences below are underlined. Replace them with a more specific word or words. Use the proofreading symbol ( ) to delete general words. Use the (⋏) symbol to insert a more specific word or words.

1. While I was home alone watching <u>a TV show</u>, I heard a <u>noise</u> in <u>another room</u>.

2. <u>One day my friend</u> and I rode our bikes <u>to a park</u>. We bought <u>something to eat and drink</u>.

3. The soccer ball cost <u>a lot</u>.

MINI-LESSON
Replace Overused Verbs

Purposes   To review the use of specific nouns (see Mini-lesson 16 page 54)

To replace the overused verbs *went* and *said* with more specific verbs

To model the use of proofreading marks to delete and insert words

Material   ◉ Individual copies of Student Activity 17 (page 57)

Teaching the Lesson

Write the following sentences on the chalkboard:

> 1) Jimmy *went* to the *store* to buy *something to eat.*
> 2) Lizzie *said*, "Help me. I'm falling!"

Review Mini-lesson 16 (see page 54). Ask your students to name the neighborhood delicatessen, market, or grocery where they buy lunch or snacks. Then ask them to name the specific foods they buy.

Show them how you use proofreading marks (⌐ and ∧) to delete the words *store* and *something to eat* in sentence #1 above and then insert the more specific words students suggested.

Tell your students that the words *went* and *said* are general verbs that don't tell the reader much. Point out that often writers replace these verbs with more specific verbs to give the reader more information. Say, "If Jimmy rode his bicycle to the store, we could write: *Jimmy bicycled to the store.*"

Ask your students for specific verbs that could replace *went*. [Possible responses: *walked; jogged; raced; ran; dashed.*]

Read the second sentence aloud and ask children to suggest more specific verbs than *said*.

Distribute copies of Student Activity 17. Explain that there is no single correct answer for each sentence and that word choices will vary.

Name _____ Date _____

Toss Out Tired Verbs

Directions: Replace the underlined verbs in the following sentences with more specific ones. Select from the box below the verb that best conveys the meaning of each sentence, or use your own ideas. Try to choose a different verb for each sentence.

Use the proofreading mark ℮ to delete words and ∧ to insert words.

1. When he heard the fire alarm, he <u>went quickly</u> down the stairs.

2. Mother <u>said</u>, "Be quiet. You'll wake the baby with that shouting."

3. "What is Mother cooking?" <u>said</u> Jan. "It smells so good."

4. My little sister fell down and <u>said</u>, "I hurt my foot!"

5. Jeff turned around to see who had pushed him. "Watch where you're going! You made me drop my books," he <u>said</u>.

6. "You prepared this lunch all by yourself," Grandmother <u>said</u>. "I can't believe it."

7. "Shh, I hear a strange noise," <u>said</u> Patty.

8. The girls <u>went</u> out of the spooky house as fast as they could.

9. Pete <u>went</u> into the pool and the race began.

10. He <u>went</u> down the hill quickly when he heard the cry, "Rock slide!"

asked	hollered	scolded	whispered
cried	hurried	scrambled	wondered
dashed	jumped	screamed	yelled
dove	raced	shouted	
exclaimed	ran	sped	
flew	rushed	warned	

MINI-LESSON 18
Using Action Verbs

Purpose To demonstrate the importance of strong, specific verbs that show the action

Material ⚙ Student Activity 18 (page 59)

Teaching the Lesson

Copy the following two excerpts from *The Hit-Away Kid* by Matt Christopher onto the chalkboard or an overhead transparency:

> *They skateboarded up the cement walk. Their wheels clacked over the cracks, and more than once Susan's board rolled off the walk. . . .*
> *"Hey Barry!" he heard a familiar voice say, and he saw his friend José sweeping around the corner on his fancy skateboard.*

> *Barry fielded the ball and whipped it to keep Dick from running there. Then Judd singled, driving in Dick. . . . Dave blasted a long fly to deep left that went foul by inches, but Barry caught it for an out.*

Tell your students that we can learn a lot about powerful, specific verbs from Matt Christopher and other sportswriters. Ask them to listen for the action words that help them see exactly what is happening as you read aloud the excerpts. Afterward, call on students to come up and underline the strong, specific verbs. [Answers: First excerpt: *skateboarded; clacked; rolled; sweeping.* Second excerpt: *fielded; whipped; running; singled; driving; blasted; caught.*]

Ask your students what someone who didn't know about specific action verbs might have used instead of *whipped* and *blasted*. [Possible responses: *threw* and *hit*.]

Say: "A specific verb puts a picture in a reader's mind. What does the verb *skateboarded* make you see?" [Possible response: *Someone riding a narrow board on wheels, arms outstretched, one foot in front of the other, knees bent.*]

Distribute Student Activity 18. [Answers: *1. squeal; 2. hunt; 3. scribbled; 4. tumbled; 5. scrambles; 6. whiz; 7. boomed; 8. roared; 9. explored; 10. crept.*]

25 MINI-LESSONS FOR TEACHING WRITING • CLARITY
Scholastic Professional Books, 1997

Specific Action Verbs

Directions: Delete the underlined action word or word group in each sentence and insert a strong, specific verb from the box below. Use the appropriate proofreading marks to make the changes.

Example: Time ~~went by slowly~~. I couldn't wait to see my friend.
                     crept

1. I heard the tires <u>make a noise</u> as the car turned the corner.

2. The lizard climbed over the walls to <u>look</u> for meal worms.

3. Jim <u>wrote</u> a short note to his mother because he was in a hurry.

4. Mike <u>fell</u> from the top rung of the ladder.

5. On Sunday my dad <u>makes</u> eggs for our breakfast.

6. The sleds really <u>go fast</u> down this hill.

7. The voice <u>came</u> loud and clear over the gym's loudspeaker.

8. The motorcycle <u>made a lot of noise</u> as it sped by.

9. I <u>walked all around</u> our new house.

10. Mary's knees shook as she and Jenny <u>walked</u> through the dark old house.

crept	scrambles	tumbled
explored	scribbled	whiz
hunt	boomed	
roared	squeal	

MINI-LESSON
Compare to Make It Clear

Purpose To describe something by comparing it to something else

Material ◉ Individual copies of Student Activity 19 (page 61)

Teaching the Lesson

Say: "Writers can create images or pictures in the reader's mind by using comparisons. In fact, most of us do this naturally when we talk. By using the words *like* or *as* to show how two different things are similar, we are creating a *simile*. For example, imagine that you are angry because someone took your bicycle without permission. What words could you use to complete this simile: *"I was as mad as a _____?"* [Possible responses: *wild dog; bee whose honey was stolen.*]

Now listen to the way Jon, a third grader, uses a simile in his writing to describe how he felt when school ended on the day he turned 10:

> *Ring, ring. It was three o'clock. I raced out of school as fast as I could. I was as free as a floating balloon. No homework; no spelling; no nothing. It was my birthday.*

Say: "Jon compares himself to a floating balloon to give his readers a clearer picture of just how lighthearted he felt. Further on in his story he uses another comparison. Listen carefully as I read so you can spot it."

> *I got my roller skates and skated outside for quite some time. I was waiting for 6:00, when my family and I would celebrate. Then I went inside. I looked at the clock. 5:30. I watched a television show. During the show I kept looking at the clock. The hands were moving as slow as molasses in January.*

Ask students the following: 1. What are the two things that Jon compared in this part? [Answer: *the clock's hands and cold molasses.*]

2. What does the comparison show about his feelings? [Possible responses: *He felt time was going so slowly. He couldn't wait until the clock said 6:00.*]

Distribute Student Activity 19. [Answers may vary. If chosen from list provided: *1. c; 2. b; 3. d; 4. j; 5. h; 6. e; 7. i; 8. f; 9. g; 10. a.*]

Name _____ Date _____

Simile Search

Directions: Below is a list of unfinished comparisons, or similes. Choose an expression from the box below to complete each simile, or create your own.

1. The ballet dancer is as graceful as _____.

2. Our classroom was as noisy as _____.

3. When I saw the blood, I turned as pale as _____.

4. My baby sister is as cuddly as _____.

5. When my parents went away on a trip, my little brother was as frantic as _____.

6. I could see Annie was getting reading to steal a base. She was bouncing on her toes like _____.

7. My little brother acted as silly as _____.

8. When I am tired, my handwriting is as crooked as _____

   _____.

9. His mother said he was as skinny as _____.

10. His eyes lit up like _____.

a) two headlights	f) a corkscrew
b) a monkey house in the zoo	g) a mouse's tail
c) a swan	h) a lost child
d) a ghost	i) a clown
e) a ballet dancer	j) a kitten

MINI-LESSON
Riddle Poems (Metaphors)

Purpose To show how poets use metaphors to describe something

Material ◉ Individual overhead copies or transparency of Student Activity 20 (page 63)

Teaching the Lesson

Say: "Writers—particularly poets—often describe something by comparing it to something else without using the words *like* or *as*. We call these word pictures *metaphors*. Listen, for example, to this metaphor poem by William Jay Smith. Try to guess its title—it shows what he is really describing."

(Your students should easily guess the poem's title—"The Toaster.")

> *A silver-scaled Dragon with jaws flaming red*
> *Sits at my elbow and toasts my bread.*
> *I hand him fat slices, and then, one by one,*
> *He hands them back when he sees they are done.*

Ask the following questions (possible responses in italics):

1 Which words helped you figure out that the poet is describing a toaster?
Toasts my bread; I hand him fat slices.

2 What do the words "A silver-scaled Dragon with jaws flaming red" make you think of?
A shiny metal toaster with electric coils that heat up and turn red; a toaster when it's hot.

Distribute copies of Student Activity 20. Project the poems using an overhead projector. Explain that each metaphor poem is like a riddle. Students will have to figure out what the word pictures really represent.

After your students complete the activity, read aloud the correct titles, as follows:

Poem 1, by Gerald Raferty: "Apartment House"
Poem 2, by James Reeves: "Fireworks"
Poem 3, by Beatrice Janosow: "The Garden Hose"

Name _____ Date _____

Guess the Subject

Directions: Guess the real subject of each poem. Write a title above each poem that tells what the poet is really describing.

1. Title: _____

> A filing cabinet of human lives
> Where people swarm like bees in tunneled hives
> Each to his own cell in the towered comb
> Identical and cramped—we call it home.
>
>   —Gerald Raferty

2. Title: _____

> They rise like sudden fiery flowers
> They burst upon the night,
> Then fall to earth in burning showers
> Of crimson, blue, and white.
> Like buds too wonderful to name,
> Each miracle unfolds,
> And Catherine-wheels begin to flame
> Like whirling marigolds.
> Rockets and Roman candles make
> An orchard of the sky,
> Whence magic trees their petals shake
> Upon each gazing eye.
>
>   —James Reeves

3. Title: _____

> In the gray evening
> I see a long, green serpent
> With its tail in the dahlias.
> It lies in loops across the grass
> And drinks softly at the faucet.
> I can hear it swallow.
>
>   —Beatrice Janosow

Clarity: Follow-It-Up

Writing

◎ Show your students how to use a thesaurus to locate more specific words: First, make a transparency of a piece of student writing that lacks specifics. Underline the general words that need to be replaced (e.g., *said, went, ran, cooked*). Then make a transparency of a thesaurus page or pages that has some of the words you've underlined on it. Ask your students to find stronger synonyms or related words on the thesaurus page that could replace the weak words in the student writing.

◎ During a writing conference, encourage students to ask each other questions such as these:

1. *Can you use a stronger verb that makes me see the action?*

2. *You say you were watching a TV show. Which one?*

3. *You write that you were feeling [mad, scared, happy, sad]. What were you thinking to yourself at the time? What did you do or say?*

Literature

◎ Read aloud stories, including picture books, that use precise and beautiful language. A few examples of picture books that do this are *Home Place* by Crescent Dragonwagon (Macmillan, 1990), Anna Egan Smucker's *No Star Nights* (Knopf, 1989), and *Home* (HarperCollins, 1992).

Following a reading, ask your students to recall lines and words that put vivid pictures in their minds.

◎ Photocopy Roald Dahl's description of The Trunchbull (in *Matilda*, Puffin Books, page 67). Provide each student with a copy, a sheet of unlined paper, and a set of crayons or markers so they can draw the headmistress as Dahl describes her.

◎ Invite your students to share additional examples of precise and vivid language that they find in the books they read on their own.

Editing

Editing is the fix-up stage in the writer's process. It's a good idea to review the conventions of writing with your students providing a checklist such as the one on page 79. Then use the mini-lessons and activities in this section to show them how to delete unnessary words, strengthen verbs, and combine short sentences. A list of proofreading marks such as the one on page 80 is useful for making editing changes.

MINI-LESSON
Use Proofreading Marks

Purpose To teach your students how to use proofreader's marks when revising and editing

Materials
- ◎ Chart or chalkboard
- ◎ Individual photocopies of Proofreading Marks chart (page 80)
- ◎ Individual copies of Student Activity 21 (page 67)

Teaching the Lesson

Explain proofreading marks by saying something like this: "Writers use proofreading marks to indicate changes they think should be made. These symbols are shortcuts to help you correct errors and make changes before you recopy work. You already are familiar with two symbols that we've used for deleting and inserting words."

Write the following deletion and insertion symbols on a chart or chalkboard:

(deletion)   (insertion)

Distribute the Proofreading Marks chart to each student and say: "You can find a complete list of proofreader's marks in many dictionaries, but you'll find basic proofreader's marks on this sheet. It's a good idea to keep this sheet in your writing folder for quick reference."

Distribute Student Activity 21 and say: "This activity will give you some practice using new symbols to make a variety of changes in your writing. Look at your Proofreading Marks sheet to find the appropriate symbol for each revision."

Name _____ Date _____

Be a Proofreading Pro

Directions: Use the appropriate proofreading mark to make each change, following the instructions below.

1. Delete the bold-faced words and insert commas before and after the words *my best friend*:

   Jim **who is** my best friend is moving to a new town.

2. Close the space between the two words that should be one word:

   My grand mother knitted this scarf for me.

3. Open the space between the words that run together:

   I've been waiting here for anhour.

4. Capitalize the first letters of the important words in the book titles:

   Linda's favorite books are harriet the spy and freckle juice.

5. Change the first letters of the bold-faced words to the lowercase:

   My little **Sister** follows me everywhere I go. I can't **Stand It!**

6. Move the first sentence to follow the second sentence:

   I put on my warmest jacket and went out. It was a cold and windy day.

7. Insert quotation marks before and after the speaker's words:

   Where have you been? asked my mother. I've been looking all over for you.

8. Start a new paragraph for the second speaker and indent the new paragraph:

   "Could I have a kitten?" I asked my dad. "You'd better ask Mom," he said.

MINI-LESSON
Edit to Strengthen Verbs

Purpose To teach two strategies for strengthening verbs:

1. Eliminate *-ing* verb endings and the accompanying forms of the verb *to be,* such as: *is, was, were, am, are.*

2. Replace weak verbs with single strong, specific verbs suggested by a simile.

Materials ◉ Chart, chalkboard, or overhead transparency

◉ Individual copies of Student Activity 22 (pages 69–70)

Teaching the Lesson

Display the following writing sample:

> ### The U.S. Open Tennis Championships
>
> *The play started and everybody sat down except us. While the pros <u>were playing</u>, Lisa and I <u>were trying</u> to find our way back to our seats. We <u>were carrying</u> Italian ices in each hand. We couldn't find our way to the right section of seats. The ices <u>were melting and dripping</u> all over us as we <u>were searching</u> for my parents.*
>
> Kim, grade 4

Explain that Kim's story is interesting, but her verbs need to be strengthened. Demonstrate how she could do this by deleting the words *were playing* in the second sentence and inserting the word *played.*

Ask your students to revise the remaining underlined word groups in the same way. [Answers: *tried; carried; melted and dripped; searched.*]

Next, display the following sentence:

The kids *came* down the steps like a herd of elephants.

Ask your students to think of a stronger verb suggested by the above comparison. [Possible responses: *stampeded, thundered, tramped.*]

Distribute Student Activity 22 [Answers: *Part A: 1. watched; 2. walked; 3. practices ; 4. met; 5. will move. Part B: Answers will vary.*]

Wanted: Strong Verbs

Directions:

A. Change each verb ending and eliminate the helping verbs *was*, *were*, *is*, and *be*.

Example: John was shoveling snow.

John shoveled snow.

1. They were watching television.

They _____ television.

2. Mike was walking to the park.

Mike _____ to the park.

3. Janie is practicing her piano lessons every day.

Janie _____ her piano lessons every day.

4. They were meeting to discuss their team's plans.

They _____ to discuss their team's plans.

5. My family will be moving to another city.

My family _____ to another city.

(continued)

Directions:

B. Replace each underlined verb with a strong, specific verb suggested by the simile (comparison).

Example: Mike <u>went through</u> the opposing team like an army tank.

Mike ___rolled___ into the opposing team like an army tank.

1. Like a drifting cloud, Julie <u>came</u> down the stairs.

   Like a drifting cloud, Julie _____ down the stairs.

2. Willie <u>moved</u> along the floor like a snake.

   Willie _____ along the floor like a snake.

3. The rain <u>came</u> onto our rooftop like a waterfall.

   The rain _____ onto our rooftop like a waterfall.

4. Our class <u>went</u> into the lunchroom like an army of hungry ants.

   Our class _____ into the lunchroom like an army of hungry ants.

5. Like a baby duck, my little sister <u>came</u> into my room.

   Like a baby duck, my little sister _____ into my room.

MINI-LESSON
Combine Short Sentences

Purposes To combine two simple sentences, forming more interesting compound sentence

To eliminate unnecessary words

Material ◉ A chart, chalkboard, or overhead transparency

◉ Individual copies of Student Activity 23 (page 72)

Teaching the Lesson

Display the following sentences on a chart, chalkboard, or transparency:

> *Liz raced down the hall. She bumped into her teacher.*

Explain that writers often combine two simple sentences such as these with a connecting word, or *conjunction*, to create a more interesting sentence.

Display the following list:

Conjunctions

although   and   as   because   but   or   so   while

Point out that sentence combining sometimes makes it possible for writers to eliminate unnecessary words and improve their writing.

Ask students to suggest ways to combine the displayed sentences by using a conjunction. Tell them that they can move words around or eliminate words. Responses will vary. Read aloud any of the following if students do not suggest them:

> *As Liz raced down the hall, she bumped into her teacher.*
> *Liz bumped into her teacher as she raced down the hall.*
> *Liz raced down the hall and bumped into her teacher.*
> *While racing down the hall, Liz bumped into her teacher.*

Distribute Student Activity 23. [Answers will vary.]

STUDENT ACTIVITY 23

Sentence Connection

Directions: Use a conjunction from the list below to combine each pair of simple sentences. You may move word groups and eliminate unnecessary words. **and   as   but   so**
although   because   or   while

1. I may jog to school. I may take the bus.

   _____

2. The bus was late. I ran to school.

   _____

3. Janie carefully planted the seeds. The flowers never bloomed.

   _____

4. The German shepherd was huge. He was a gentle dog.

   _____

5. Max hated the broccoli. He dumped it into the sink.

   _____

6. They were watching *Star Trek* on TV. They heard a crash.

   _____

7. We were walking to the movie theater. We saw two cars crash.

   _____

8. I was still hungry. I had eaten a huge lunch.

   _____

9. Cindy was tired. She was hungry. She was glad to get home.

   _____

10. I sighed happily. I closed my eyes. The sailboat glided over the
    water.

   _____

25 MINI-LESSONS FOR TEACHING WRITING • EDITING
Scholastic Professional Books, 1997

Name _____ Date _____

Sentence-Combining Challenge

Directions: Revise the two sentence groups below by combining the short, choppy sentences. Write your new sentences on the lines below each group. Use any of the following strategies:

   a) Delete unnecessary and overused words.

   b) Add conjunctions, or connecting words.

   c) Move words around.

   d) Use a series of adjectives (descriptive words).
      For example: The shirt has red, white, and blue stripes.

1. I found a shell on the beach. It is pretty. The inside is pink. It is shiny, too. The outside of the shell is rough. It has ridges. The ridges are sharp.

   _____

   _____

   _____

2. My little sister was born last Thursday. Her name is Melissa. She is pretty. She has big blue eyes. She has straight black hair. She has soft skin. She has red cheeks. Melissa is tiny. Her fingers are tiny. Her toes are tiny. Her clothes are tiny, too. They are not much bigger than a doll's.

   _____

   _____

   _____

Writing Tip: Sometimes writers purposely use short sentences to create pace and interest. For example: Judy Blume's book *Freckle Juice* begins this way: "Andrew Marcus wanted freckles. Nicky Lane had freckles. He had about a million of them."

 **MINI-LESSON**

Revising Run-On Sentences

Purpose To recognize and correct run-on sentences

Materials
- ◉ Individual copies of Student Activity 24 (page 75)
- ◉ A chart, chalkboard, or overhead transparency for displaying the example of a run-on sentence
- ◉ Lined paper and a pencil for each student

Teaching the Lesson

Display the following example of a run-on sentence:

> *Some people call diving beetles water tigers they will just grab an insect and swallow it.*

Say: "A run-on sentence occurs when two or more simple sentences are joined without punctuation or a connecting word. Look at this run-on sentence and think about various ways to correct it. Whatever strategy you use, try to eliminate unnecessary words if possible. Write your revised sentence on the lined paper." [Responses will vary.]

Distribute Student Activity 24.

Read and discuss the strategies for correcting run-on sentences and the examples provided for each strategy.

Possible revisions of the run-on sentences in Student Activity 24:

1. *On Saturday my sister and I were raking leaves. We found a chocolate bar she lost last summer.*

   While raking leaves on Saturday, my sister and I found a chocolate bar she lost last summer.

2. *At Chocolate World we saw how they poured the melted chocolate into molds. I felt like sticking my hand in and licking it because the chocolate looked so good.*

   While at Chocolate World we saw melted chocolate poured into molds. It looked so good! I felt like sticking my hand in the chocolate and licking it.

Name _____ Date _____

Fix Up the Run-On

Directions:

1. Read the following run-on sentence: *Some people call diving beetles water tigers they will just grab an insect and swallow it.* 2. Below are some strategies to fix a run-on sentence.

Create new sentences by adding periods and using capital letters.

Example: *Some people call diving beetles water tigers. They will just grab an insect and swallow it.*

Add a connecting word such as *and, although, but, so, while, as, when, because, or before.*

Example: *Some people call diving beetles water tigers because they will just grab an insect and swallow it.*

Move words around and eliminate unnecessary words.

Example: *Because they grab and swallow insects, diving beetles are sometimes called water tigers.*

Now it's your turn to fix the run-ons. Revise the following run-on sentences, using any strategies listed above.

1. On Saturday my sister and I were raking leaves we found her lost chocolate bar.

   _____

   _____

2. I visited Chocolate World we saw how they poured the melted chocolate into molds it looked so good I felt like sticking my hand in the chocolate and licking it.

   _____

   _____

MINI–LESSON
Punctuate the Dialogue

Purposes To identify dialogue by locating "speaker tags" (e.g., *said*, *asked*)

To use quotation marks and punctuation in written dialogue

To use a new paragraph for each speaker

Materials ◎ Chart or transparency for displaying example of dialogue

◎ Individual copies of Student Activity 25 (pages 77–78)

Teaching the Lesson

Display the following dialogue and ask a student to read it aloud:

> *"Jimmy," said Coach Wilson, "You're at bat next."*
>
> *"Wasn't I supposed to be up fourth?" Jimmy asked.*
>
> *"I've changed the batting order," the coach replied. "You're up now."*
>
> *So Jimmy picked up his bat and marched to the plate.*
>
> *Robert, the team captain, was behind the batting screen as Jimmy reached the plate. "You're not up yet. Go back!" he yelled.*
>
> *"That's what you think," said Jimmy. "But it's not what Coach Wilson thinks. Go and ask him yourself."*
>
> *"You bet I will!" exclaimed Robert as he stomped off toward the coach's bench.*

Ask:

1 Who are the different speakers in this dialogue?
[Answers: *Coach Wilson, Jimmy, Robert.*]

2 What words, or "speaker tags," tell us that someone is talking?
[Answers: *said, asked, replied, yelled, exclaimed.*]

Circle the speaker tags as students name them. Then explain, "Each tag helps us locate the speaker's words."

Invite students to underline the speakers' words. Then say, "These words are always separated from the rest of the sentence with opening and closing quotation marks. Look at the lines where the dialogue is first and the speaker tag is last. What other kinds of punctuation do you see before the closing quotation marks?" [Answers: *exclamation point, question mark, comma.*]

Point out that there is a separate paragraph for each speaker.

Distribute Student Activity 25.

Name _____   Date _____

Punctuation Practice

Directions: The following excerpt from Daniel's story, "The Last Risk We Took," needs editing. See if you can fix the dialogue with correct punctuation and capitalization.

Read these tips before you begin:

Tips on How to Edit Dialogue

1. Read the story.
2. Locate the speaker tags (*said, exclaimed, shouted, returned, screamed*).
3. Underline the speaker's words very lightly in pencil.
4. Put quotation marks around the speaker's exact words.
5. Capitalize the first word the speaker says.
6. Insert additional punctuation (, . ? !) before the closing quotation marks.

One day Peter and I went to the pond next to his house to see if it was frozen. It was, and we started breaking the ice up into puddles. I picked up a piece of broken ice. It was hollow inside. wow I said. look at this, Peter.

Cool said Peter.

A woman with two huge dogs walked by on the other side of the pond.

You shouldn't be doing that shouted the woman.

It's none of your business exclaimed Peter.

(continued)

The chase was on! We ran away from the pond, up some steps, through a path, and up the hill into the woods.

I think we lost her I said panting and puffing. I went down the path to check.

She's coming exclaimed Peter.

Yeah, right I returned calmly.

I'm not kidding Peter said, annoyed. Then he screamed

D A N I E L

He wasn't lying!

Ahhh I screamed as I ran to him. You can stay but I'm saving myself I shouted as I climbed the rocks.

Writing Tip:

When writing dialogue in your own story, be sure to change paragraphs when you change speakers.

Editing: Follow-It-Up

Create checklists, such as the one below, that focus on the editing skills you have taught in your mini-lessons. Tell your students to use the checklists to edit a completed writing draft—first by themselves, then with a partner. You can do a final editing check before the student recopies the work.

My Sentences:

1. use strong verbs and specific nouns;

2. are not run-ons;

3. do not use overused or unnecessary words;

4. begin with a capital letter;

5. use commas and quotation marks appropriately;

6. end with a period, question mark, or exclamation point;

7. are grouped in paragraphs with a new paragraph for each change of subject or speaker.

Together with your students, develop a list of rules for a particular editing skill, such as capitalizing words, using commas, correcting run-on sentences, or basic spelling rules. Display the rules on charts or photocopy them and have students place them in a folder for easy reference. Provide dictionaries for checking spellings, and show students how to use guide words and pronunciation keys.

Teach your students how to use proofreader's marks—symbols to indicate changes they think should be made. These symbols can help your students correct errors and revise before recopying their work. You can find a complete list of proofreader's marks in many dictionaries. It's a good idea to photocopy a list of the most common ones for each student. An example of a chart of basic proofreader's marks appears on the following page.

Teacher Tip: A perfect paper is rare. Even after a draft has been proofread, a few errors may still appear in the final, recopied piece. If the story is to be published, point out remaining errors and help the student correct them.

Proofreading Marks

Mark	Meaning	Example
℘	Delete words, sentences, and punctuation marks.	a ~~very~~ wonderful day
∧	Insert letters, words, or sentences.	chocolate I like ∧ ice cream.
#	Make a space.	Cars passed⌄by.
‿	Close a space.	grand ⌢ father
≡	Make the letter a capital.	mr. Jones
/	Make the letter lower case.	My /Brother fell.
¶	Start a new paragraph. Indent the paragraph.	"Hi, guys," he called. "Hi," we answered.
↶	Move where shown.	The final score was 6–4. I He pitched the last two innings
⌄⌄ ⌄⌄	Insert quotation marks.	Come in, she called.

Story Bank

One of the best ways to help children understand the elements of good writing is to let them hear and read good writing by other students. Many of the lessons in this book refer you to a particular story that illustrates the point of the lesson. Ask children to listen carefully so they can comment on the strategies or techniques the writer has used. As your students grow as writers be sure to add their stories to the Story Bank.

No Thanksgiving Play for Me

"Can I go to school tomorrow?" I asked my mom. "My cough is almost gone."

"We'll see," she said. But by the way she said it, it sounded like no.

The next morning I woke up to see kids walking to school. I knew there would be no Thanksgiving play for me. As the day dragged by I wanted to call Christine to see if it had gone well.

"I can call Christine now!" I thought. "It's three-thirty. She has to be home!"

But what she told me made me not glad. "It was terrific!" she told me.

That made me angry. The play wasn't supposed to go well without me. By the end of the phone call I felt like crying. I hated my class for doing well. I hated my mom for not letting me go. Most of all I hated Kate for getting my favorite line and my solo.

Of course, I've calmed down a lot since fifth grade, but whenever I look back on that day I always think, "Why did it have to be me?"

Danny, grade 6

He's a Girl!

"I want the small one," I said to the guy at the pet shop as I picked out a nice-sized diamondback turtle. It was a good size for my aquarium at home. The man put the turtle in a box and gave me a filter.

"What does it eat?" I asked.

"Goldfish," he said. "You have to buy eight a week. They cost a dollar."

"Hey, Mom, look what I have," I said as I ran through the door.

"Aaaaah!" she screamed.

I ran upstairs to prepare his home.

I got a piece of Styrofoam a little bit bigger than the width of the aquarium so that it would be higher than the water. It was like a piece of land. I added gravel. Then I put rocks in as a staircase to the land. I put the filter in. Finally I put fake aquarium plants in. I was finished at last.

"I need a name for him. Dribble!" I decided.

I put Dribble in the aquarium. He loved it! He swam, crawled up on land, and even stayed underwater for seven minutes.

"Hey, Mom, he likes the aquarium," I yelled.

A week later my mom bought a book about turtles. I looked up the chapter "What Turtles Eat."

"Hey, he eats worms, dog food, and raw table meat. The guy at the pet shop tried to rip me off at a dollar a goldfish!"

I could dig for worms anytime, I thought. "There," I said as I put three worms in the aquarium. Dribble ate one. Dirt from inside the worm spread all over the gravel. Yuuch. I never fed him worms again.

I tried feeding him dog food. I crunched three pieces with a fork. I put them in the aquarium. Dribble ate them all up.

"From now on it's dog food," I said.

Three days later I walked upstairs after school and looked in Dribble's tank. There were eight eggs. That taught me another thing: HE's a girl!

Matt, grade 5

Last One-Digit Age

Ring! Ring! I looked at the clock. It was three o'clock. I raced out of school and ran home as fast as I could. I was as free as a floating balloon. No homework, no spelling, no nothing. It was my tenth birthday.

I got my roller skates. I skated outside for quite some time. I had been waiting for six o'clock to come because my family and I would celebrate.

Then I went inside. I looked at the clock: Five-thirty. I watched a television show. During the show I kept looking at the clock. It was moving as slowly as molasses in January. Suddenly my mother called me and said, "Jon, dinnertime."

She had made my favorite foods—hamburgers and french fries. I had seconds. Just when I was finished, everyone sang, "Happy birthday." After the family had cake, I said, "This is one of the happiest days in my life."

Jon, grade 4

Max

When I was six, I was going to get my first pet. I felt so excited that I didn't know what dog to pick. I wanted a German shepherd, but they bite. My mom wanted a black Lab. We got a mutt. It was a German shepherd and black Lab. I named him Max after my favorite toy robot.

The next day, I called the dog like this: "Come Max!" Then he came. He liked his name a lot. He looked so "puppy-dog-gish." I told him to get on the bed, then off, and on the bed again. He went to the bathroom. Yuck! I told my mom so she cleaned the linen.

Since it was so hot, we wanted Max to swim in the plastic pool. Max would put his paws on the rim of the pool, but that was it. Sometimes we pushed him into the pool, but he would always climb out.

Max is not just a pet, he's a brother. He follows me everywhere if I tell him to. But the most important thing is that we love each other.

Peter, grade 4

Stuck in the Bathroom

Once my friend Lauren and I were playing in the bathroom. We locked the bathroom door so my brother would not get in. My mom yelled that it was time to wash up for dinner. When I tried to open the door, the doorknob was in my hand. I tried to jam it back on, but it was hopeless. I was really scared and so was Lauren. I thought I would never get out. I thought we would be there for two weeks without food. Personally, I thought I was going to die.

I looked out the window. I wanted to jump. Lauren would not let me. She thought I would kill myself because we were on the second floor. I knew she was right, but I was mad and scared at the same time.

We thought nobody would realize we were gone, but suddenly we heard a voice calling us. We yelled for help as loud as we could. My dad marched up with a screwdriver and the door swung open.

"We're free! We're free!" Lauren and I kept yelling. We both ran to my dad and gave him a hug.

Rachel, grade 4

Scholastic Professional Books, 1997

 # Crab Hunting

"I see a crab," I yelled to my brother, Eric. He handed me the cup. I took the cup and tried to scoop up the crab. I missed that crab, but soon I saw another crab. I yelled again and Eric handed me the cup again. I tried to scoop up the crab, but I missed it again. We did that for two hours and gave up.

When we were walking to our house, we saw something on the ground. It was a sand crab.

"I've got it," I said.

I put some sand in a cup and some water in, too. Then I put in the sand crab. The crab was two inches long and that's not a lot for a crab. My brother said, "All that for nothing."

I was excited because I found the crab. I could hold it and it wouldn't bite me. Sometimes it dropped on the floor and it was hard to find because it was the same color as the rug.

Then I went outside with Eric again. We were going toward the rocks when I saw something. "I see a crab!"

Eric yelled, "I see a crab, too!"

We both picked up our crabs. "Now we've got two more," I said. We put them in the cup, too. Now we had three!

Greg, grade 4

The Day I Broke My Finger

I was playing in the snow one day with my sister Debby. I was sliding down a hill and I put my hand deep in the snow to stop the sled. When I took it out, my pinky was bent. But it didn't hurt. Finally Debby came down to see what happened. Then she started going crazy yelling how gross it was. When I went inside, my mother screamed, too. Finally she called the hospital and told the secretary that she thought it was a broken finger.

It was a very long trip to the hospital because it was snowing and there was a traffic jam. My mom told me all about how her sister broke a finger once. When we opened the car door, a gust of wind came in the car, and when we stepped out of the car, it felt like it was a foot of snow.

When we got into the hospital, the nurse told us to go to the emergency room. It was a long wait so my mother tested me on the six times table. Then the nurse came and x-rayed my finger about five times. The doctor looked at the X ray. The finger was broken, so they got a bandage and wrapped it around my pinky and the finger next to it. They put a weird thing on me so I could keep my finger up. Then we went home. It was snowing, snowing.

Lisa, grade 3

25 MINI-LESSONS FOR TEACHING WRITING • STORY BANK
Scholastic Professional Books, 1997

The Wedding Day!

It was my aunt's wedding day! And the wedding was at my house! And my house has a lot of arches, and the one in the living room was the one they got married under. And I was the flower girl!

My aunt looked really pretty, I think. She was wearing a white silk dress with a pink ribbon around her waist. Her veil was attached to flowers in her hair. And my uncle was wearing a black suit and a white shirt.

There was a photographer and he was taking pictures of almost everybody. While my uncle and aunt were inside, my aunt's friend had a bowl of rice and gave some to everybody. And when my aunt and uncle came out, everybody threw the rice at them! My aunt and uncle said to follow them to where the reception was.

The wedding cake was beautiful! It said "Stairway to the Stars," and the icing was white with brown, green, and yellow decorations. The cake tasted so good. The reception went on from 2:00 p.m. to 10:00 p.m.

It was a SUPER day!

Elizabeth, grade 3

Baby Melissa

My new baby sister, Melissa, came home from the hospital on Thursday. She is tiny and pretty. She has big blue eyes, straight black hair, and soft skin. She has red cheeks, too. Her fingers and toes are tiny, and her clothes aren't much bigger than a big doll's.

She likes to eat and sleep and cry. She likes the color red but she hates noise. She doesn't like it when a loud noise wakes her up.

She had a test at the hospital. When they gave her a shot in the heel, she cried once. They put a Band-Aid on her heel.

When I come home from school, I like to play with her. If I talk to her, she smiles. Sometimes I get to hold her. It is fun. My mom says to hold her head up.

I can hardly wait for her to be four years old so we can play together.

Edward, grade 3

Scholastic Professional Books, 1997

Being the Baby

Being the baby in the family has its advantages. But sometimes it's terrible! Like one day I was just sitting in my big brother David's room. He was in there too with his friend Brian. He turned on his radio.

Brian said, "Bye, Laura."

I said, "Where am I going?"

"Leave," said David.

"No," I said.

"Take a hike, Laura."

"No, no, no!" I felt David push me out the door.

"Mom!" I yelled. David kicked me out of his room.

"Leave Dave alone. OK?" said my mom.

"OK," I said.

That is the bad part. But here is the good part. My brother David was saving up for a stuffed beaver named Bentley, the Dog. He got it. I felt left out. I told my mom I wanted a stuffed animal too. We went to the attic and got me a stuffed monkey. I named him Marvin Monkey.

Those are the advantages when you are the baby in the family.

Laura, grade 3

The Breaks of Sailing

The orange boat glided leisurely across the water. I watched the sail billowing out like a fat giant's body. The sun beat on me, soaking me in its bright warm rays.

My friend, Jon, yawned and burped as he turned over on the bow of the 12-foot sailboat. We were on a saltwater lake in Rhode Island on our maiden voyage.

I sighed happily and closed my eyes feeling very relaxed, but maybe a little too relaxed. For the next thing I knew, a powerful gust of wind caught our sail, whipping it to an almost vertical tilt. Before we could do anything to right the vessel, I heard a loud thud and the boat capsized, pitching me headfirst into the water.

I groaned in agony as my face hit the water in a huge belly whop. I gasped for breath as the salt water filled my eyes. I surfaced and wiped my eyes clear of the salt water, and the pain from the salt water stung. On the verge of tears, I glanced over to the boat, which was half filled with water, but there was no damage except that our gear had floated away. And then I looked at my friend. His hair was wet and looked as if he just fell from a loft building. My friend was swimming toward the boat.

"Are you all right?" I queried.

"Yes," he answered.

We stood up on the sandbar, grabbed the edge of the boat jutting out of the water, placed our feet in the wet sand, and pulled till our arms ached and our backs hurt.

Twenty minutes later the boat was righted but filled with water. We bailed it out by splashing the water with our hands and feet.

When we finished, we shoved the boat off the sandbar and boarded it. Then, catching the wind in our sail, my wet crewman and I set off with the wind.

Nathan, grade 6

The Diving Beetle

Down it dives with a bubble captured under its wing. What is it? A diving beetle of course, named for the way it moves through the water.

A baby diving beetle is called a larva. Some people call them water tigers because of their terrible habits. They will just grab any insect, even insects larger than themselves. The beetle breaks open its jaws and swallows.

When the larva grows a little it makes itself a little kind of a crib underground with a hard bottom. It goes into its crib upside down. After a few months, it comes out from the bottom of the crib with a hard shell. It is a grown-up now and can dive down through the water.

The diving beetle eats algae and other pond plants. If you go to a pond or a stream you will probably find it in the algae or duckweed.

Nicole, Grade 4

The Whirligig Beetle

He's swift, he jumps, he turns and is known as the whirligig beetle. He dives down and then comes up again when it's safe and no animals can hurt him.

He has a fan-shaped middle and long legs. He is shaped like this so he can swim and dive. He has four eyes, two above and two below the water. The upper eyes see the surface and the lower eyes see the water and everything under the surface.

The babies are vicious because they swish and they swash and they scamper around. During winter whirligig beetles get out of the water and hide under the leaves until winter ends. Also during winter they eat other insects, meat, and can be kept in an aquarium.

There are more than 50 kinds of these beetles in the U.S.A.! They also smell horrible, so don't try catching one!

Michael, grade 4

Tying Up the Game

"Dribble, Dave, dribble!" I screamed. We were losing the soccer game 2–1 against Fox Meadow. Boy! Was I mad!

With about 50 seconds left, David intercepted a pass and dribbled the ball downfield toward Fox Meadow's goal. Suddenly my hopes shot up. I plunged into the center.

"Pass, Dave, pass!" I cried.

David looked up. He saw me and passed. I slid. My right foot met the ball. The wind made the dust fly in the air. I shut my eyes. Did I score?

I opened my eyes and saw the team rushing toward me and cheering. I felt so good. I tied the game up with 43 seconds left in the game. I tried hard not to smile because everybody would think I was showing off. But it was hard not to smile because I was so happy.

Sadi, grade 6

Student Revision: First and Final Drafts

Fatalean

First Draft

I was five years old when I was going to feed my mother's horse a section of hay but before I got in the stall the door slid open, and the horse walked out of the stall and not seeing me accidentally knocked me over.

Final Draft

One day when I was only five years old, I was up at my mother's country house with my brother. My mother was going to the farm to feed all the horses.

"Can I go with you?" I asked excitedly.

"Yes, but be good or I'll throw you out of the barn," she told me.

"OK!" I said, excitedly again.

When we got to the barn, I looked at all the horses. They were all pretty. Then my mother began to give each horse a section of hay.

I asked her, "Mom, can I feed him?"

"Yes, now take the hay while I get her."

But she didn't say she was about to bring the horse outside so I could feed it. She opened the stall slowly. The big brown pregnant horse Fatalean wobbled out while I charged in. We hit! My head to her chest. I fell to the concrete flat on my stomach. Fatalean walked right over the top of me.

I screamed and cried, "Mom! Help! The horse is going to kill me!"

Frightened, the horse ran outside and my mother came over to me while her friend went to catch the horse.

"Are you OK?" asked my mom.

"Yes-s-s-s," I said, frightened. After that accident I was scared of horses for a couple of months. Then they became my favorite animal.
Jayme, Grade 6

Scholastic Professional Books, 1997